curious about
EASTER

BY AMY HOUTS

AMICUS LEARNING

What are you

CHAPTER ONE

A Spring Holiday
PAGE
4

CHAPTER TWO

The History of Easter
PAGE
10

curious about?

CHAPTER THREE

Let's Celebrate!
PAGE **14**

Stay Curious! Learn More . . . 22
Glossary 24
Index 24

Curious About is published by
Amicus Learning, an imprint of Amicus
P.O. Box 227, Mankato, MN 56002
www.amicuspublishing.us

Copyright © 2026 Amicus.
International copyright reserved in all countries.
No part of this book may be reproduced in any form without written permission from the publisher.

Editor: Ana Brauer
Series Designer: Kathleen Petelinsek
Book Designer and Photo Researcher: Sara Hood

Library of Congress Cataloging-in-Publication Data
Names: Houts, Amy, 1957– author.
Title: Curious about Easter / by Amy Houts.
Description: Mankato, MN : Amicus Learning, an imprint of Amicus, [2026] | Series: Curious about holidays | Includes bibliographical references and index. | Audience: Ages 6–9 | Audience: Grades 2–3 | Summary: "Discover the magic of Easter! Learn about Easter's significance, traditions, and history in this question-and-answer book for elementary-aged readers. Includes table of contents, glossary, further resources, and index"—Provided by publisher.
Identifiers: LCCN 2025014076 (print) | LCCN 2025014077 (ebook) | ISBN 9798892008457 (library binding) | ISBN 9798892009119 (paperback) | ISBN 9798892009775 (ebook)
Subjects: LCSH: Easter—Juvenile literature.
Classification: LCC GT4935 .H687 2026 (print) | LCC GT4935 (ebook) | DDC 394.2667—dc23/eng/20250512
LC record available at https://lccn.loc.gov/2025014076
LC ebook record available at https://lccn.loc.gov/2025014077

Photo Credits: Alamy Stock Photo/Megapress, 21; Freepik/ElenaMedvedeva, 4; Getty Images/Grant Faint, 20, Hiya Images/Corbis/VCG, 14–15, imageBROKER/Anja Uhlemeyer-Wrona, 13, Looks Like Me, 2, 6–7, Senko Nelly, 17, Soeren Stache/picture alliance, 3, 18–19, Shutterstock/Jag_cz, cover, 1, jorisvo, 8, Lindasj22, 5, Romolo Tavani, 9; The Noun Project/Neneng Yuliani Lestari, 23, Solid Icon Co, 22, 23; Wikimedia Commons/Leonardo da Vinci, 2, 10–11

Every effort has been made to contact copyright holders for material reproduced in this book. Any omissions will be rectified in subsequent printings if notice is given to the publisher.

CHAPTER ONE
1

A SPRING HOLIDAY

What is Easter?

Easter is a spring holiday. Leaves bud and flowers bloom in spring. New life is a sign of spring. It's a sign of Easter, too. People celebrate the **resurrection** of Jesus. This holiday is a "holy day."

Easter reminds us that Jesus died on the cross.

Jesus was buried in a tomb like this one near Jerusalem, Israel.

A SPRING HOLIDAY

Who celebrates Easter?

Anyone can celebrate Easter.

DID YOU KNOW?
About 8 out of 10 Americans celebrate Easter.

A SPRING HOLIDAY

Christians celebrate Easter. But some people who are not Christian do, too. People of all ages can take part. They live in countries all over the world. Some people celebrate Easter like people do in the United States. Other people celebrate in different ways.

A SPRING HOLIDAY

Why do people celebrate Easter?

Easter is the most important Christian holiday. Christians believe Jesus is God's son. They are sad that he died on Good Friday. Three days later, he came back to life. Christians are happy because he lives again. Celebrating Easter gives people hope.

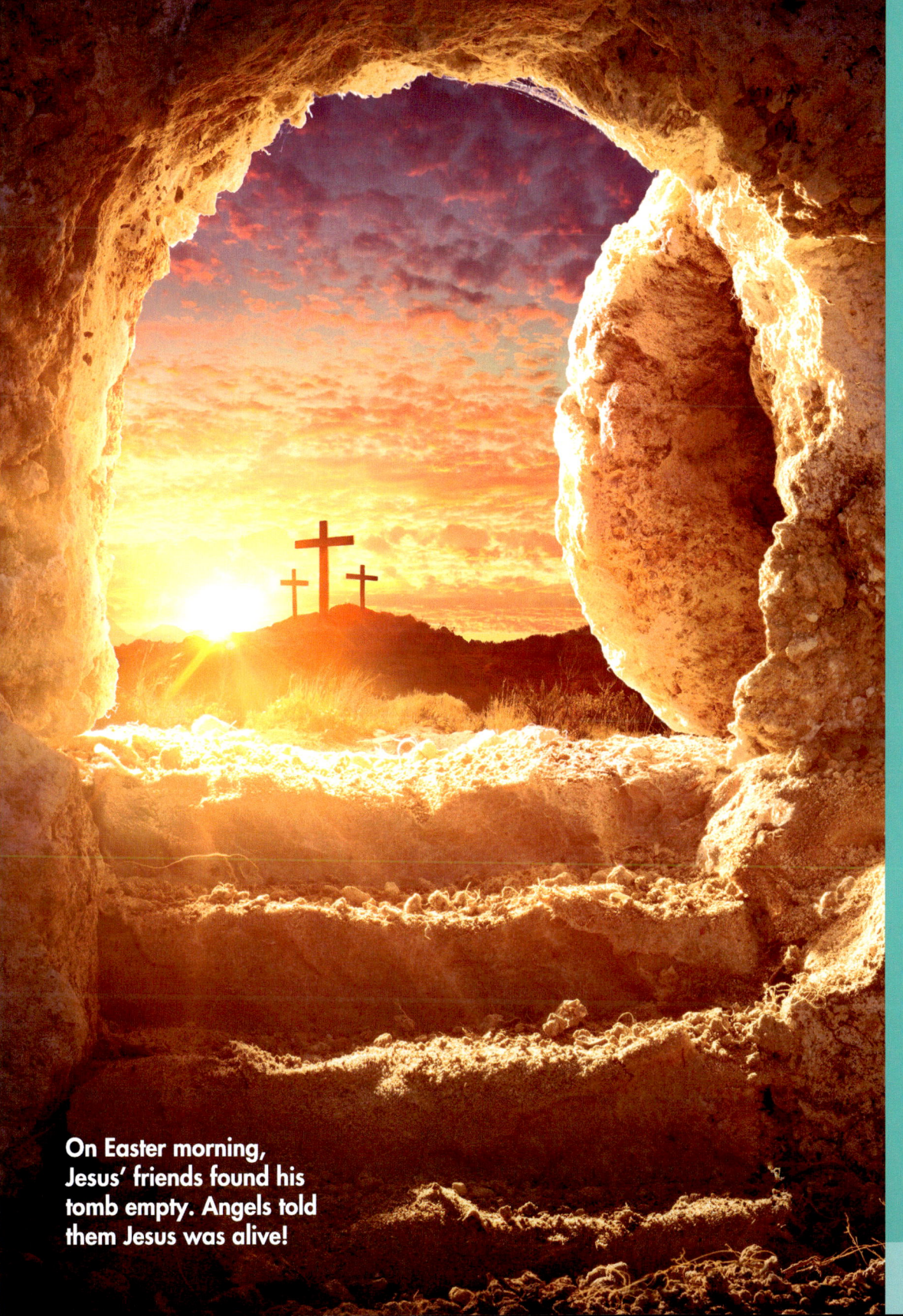

On Easter morning, Jesus' friends found his tomb empty. Angels told them Jesus was alive!

A SPRING HOLIDAY

CHAPTER TWO

How long has Easter been celebrated?

THE HISTORY OF EASTER

DID YOU KNOW?
Jesus ate with his 12 **disciples** the day before he died on the cross.

Christians have celebrated Easter for a long time. It's a very old holiday. Jesus died around 33 A.D. People in Jerusalem started celebrating Easter around 200 A.D. Easter has been a holiday for nearly 2,000 years!

The Last Supper was painted by Leonardo da Vinci in the late 1400s.

When do people celebrate Easter?

Easter has a different date each year. First, you need to know when spring starts. It starts around March 19, 20, or 21. This is called the spring **equinox**, when day and night are about the same. Look for the full moon after that. Easter is the next Sunday.

Easter is celebrated in spring when flowers start to bloom.

THE HISTORY OF EASTER

DID YOU KNOW?
Easter can be anytime from March 22 to April 25.

CHAPTER THREE

What do people do for Easter?

Some Christians prepare for Easter during a time called **Lent**. It lasts for 40 days. They give up something like candy. Lent ends during **Holy Week**. Eggs are another big part of Easter. People **dye** hard-boiled eggs different colors.

Easter eggs are dyed to celebrate spring.

LET'S CELEBRATE!

DID YOU KNOW?
Many Christians don't eat meat on Fridays during Lent. This is to honor Jesus' **sacrifice** on Good Friday.

How do people celebrate Easter?

The Easter Bunny leaves a basket filled with candy or presents. Many Christians get dressed up to go to church. They celebrate Jesus' life. People often gather with family to eat a big meal. Young kids often join an Easter egg hunt.

Easter egg hunts are a fun way to celebrate the holiday.

LET'S CELEBRATE!

Where is the Easter Bunny from?

Settlers from Germany brought the Easter Bunny **tradition** to America. The Easter Bunny decorates eggs. He leaves them in baskets for children. People have egg hunts. An egg is a symbol of new life.

In Germany, people decorate Easter eggs with detailed, colorful patterns.

How do people celebrate Easter in Mexico?

Some people make crosses out of palm leaves.

LET'S CELEBRATE!

Holy week is called "Semana Santa." People decorate with flowers and palm-leaf crosses. They act out the last days of Jesus' life. These events are quiet and sad. But they end with joy on Easter.

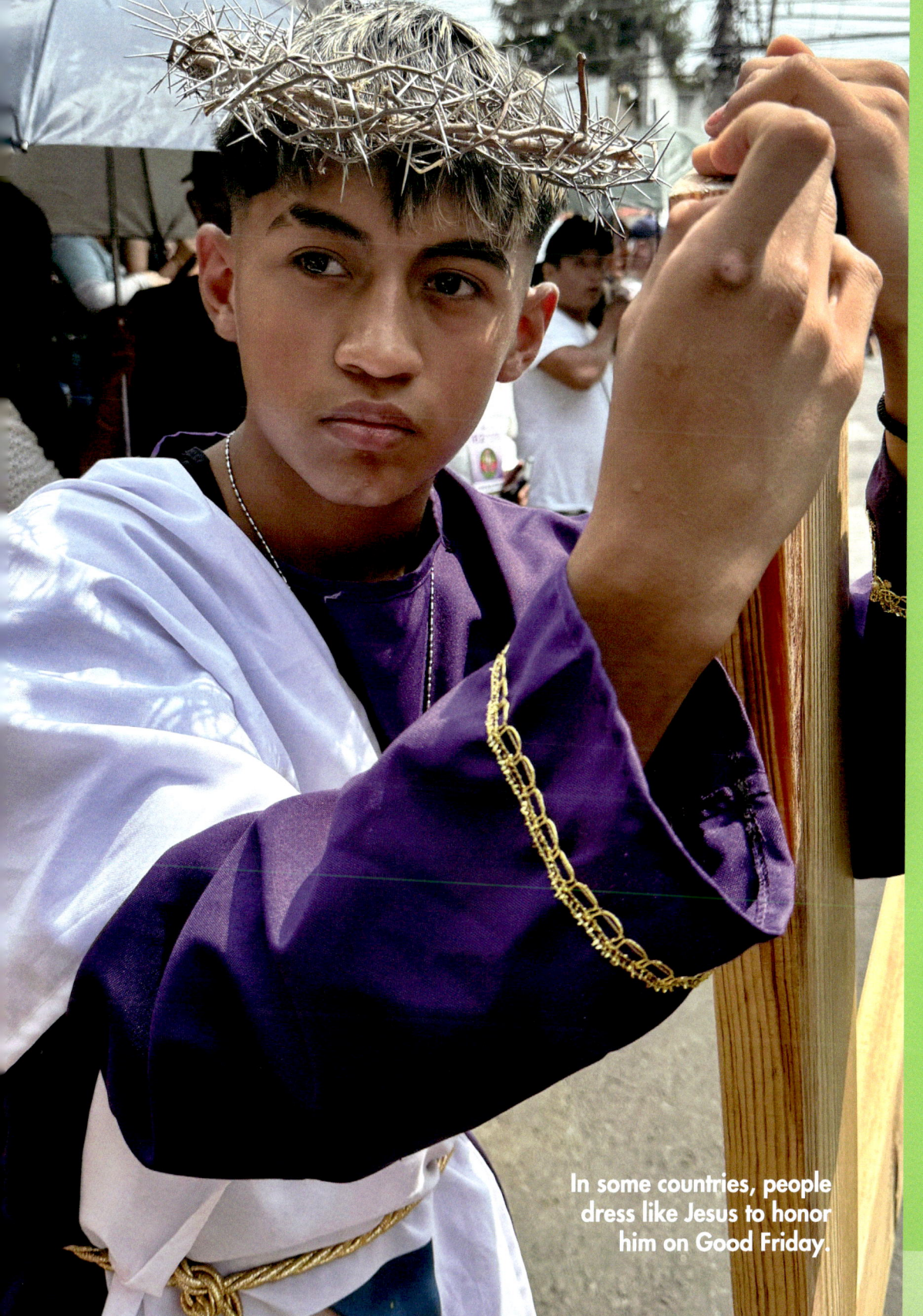

In some countries, people dress like Jesus to honor him on Good Friday.

LET'S CELEBRATE!

STAY CURIOUS!

ASK MORE QUESTIONS

How is Easter celebrated in other countries?

What do people eat for Easter dinner?

Try a BIG QUESTION: Why do people give up things for Lent?

SEARCH FOR ANSWERS

Search the library catalog or the Internet.
A librarian, teacher, or parent can help you.

Using Keywords
Find the looking glass.

Keywords are the most important words in your question.

If you want to know about:
- Easter celebrations in other countries, type: EASTER WORLD CELEBRATIONS
- Easter food, type: EASTER DINNER

LEARN MORE

FIND GOOD SOURCES

Here are some good, safe sources you can use in your research.
Your librarian can help you find more.

Books

Easter Traditions Around the World
by M. J. Cosson, 2022.

Rise: A Child's Guide to Eastertide
by Laura Alary, 2025.

Internet Sites

Britannica Kids | Easter
https://kids.britannica.com/kids/article/Easter/353077
This site provides information about Easter and how Christians prepare for it.

Kiddle | Easter Facts for Kids
https://kids.kiddle.co/Easter
Kiddle is an online encyclopedia for kids. Search for facts about Easter.

Every effort has been made to ensure that these websites are appropriate for children. However, because of the nature of the Internet, it is impossible to guarantee that these sites will remain active indefinitely or that their contents will not be altered.

SHARE AND TAKE ACTION

Dye Easter eggs.
Ask an adult to help you make hard-boiled eggs and mix up the dyes.

Have an Easter egg hunt. Ask someone to hide eggs.
Ask a friend to join you. You can gather eggs in a basket or pail.

Prepare special Easter food. Find a recipe online.
Have a parent or guardian help you.

GLOSSARY

disciple A person who accepts and helps to spread the teachings of another.

dye To add color to eggs, clothing, or hair.

equinox One of two days each year, in March and September, when day and night are the same length of time.

Holy Week The week leading up to Easter.

Lent Forty days before Easter. Starts on Ash Wednesday and ends during Holy Week.

resurrection A return to life after death.

sacrifice The act of giving up something of great value to show loyalty or deep affection.

tradition The handing down of information, beliefs, and customs from parents to children over many years.

INDEX

baskets, 16, 19
Christians, 7, 8, 11, 14, 15, 16
church, 16
Easter Bunny, 16, 18–19
eggs, 14, 15, 16, 17, 19
equinox, 12
Jesus, 4, 5, 8, 9, 10, 11, 15, 16, 20, 21
Last Supper, The, 11
Lent, 14, 15
Mexico, 20–21
resurrection, 4, 8–9
spring, 4, 12, 13, 15

About the Author

Amy Houts is the author of more than 100 picture books. Amy has celebrated Easter since she was a little girl. Now she's a grandmother! She loves writing about holidays. When Amy is not writing, you can find her walking her dog in Northwest Missouri.